CADENCE
OF
LIFE

8 Traits For Winning In And Out Of The Classroom

FEDRICK INGRAM

with
Carla DuPont

Cadence of Life
Copyright © 2018
ISBN: 978-0-578-40803-3

All rights reserved. In accordance with the U.S. Copyright Act of 1976, the scanning, uploading, and electronic sharing of any part of this book without the permission of the publisher constitutes unlawful piracy and theft of the author's intellectual property. If you would like to use material from the book (other than for review purposes), prior written permission must be obtained by contacting Fedrick Ingram using fedingram@hotmail.com. Thank you for supporting the author's rights.

Credits
Editorial: Constance Poitier
Cover Design: Garrett Myers
Interior Design: Carla DuPont

DEDICATION

This book is written in honor of my family; we are an American story of struggle, perseverance, pain, and progress. A family whose unrelenting faith in God has held together generations of hardships juxtaposed by a southern ideology of oppression, separatism, political and economic idealism that promoted the haves away from the have nots. Through it all, we are still here pressing forward and making this world a better place. I am one generation removed from grandparents on my maternal and paternal sides with no formal education. In fact, reading and writing was not afforded to them in an educational setting; what little they could understand was taught to them many years into adulthood by their own children. The way of the world for them in the south was the sun. Sun up, you went to work. Sun down, you went to sleep. You repeated that effort from a very early age into adulthood.

They are somewhere in heaven laughing with joy probably saying, 'Look at what we did!' Grandchildren, great-grandchildren and great-great grandchildren who have become educators, lawyers, doctors, professional athletes, professional dancers, leaders in business, education, politics, and entertainment. I'm proud to be a first generation college graduate, third generation Floridian, and seventh generation American whose family is of African descent.

My parents never taught my three brothers and I how to live; they lived and gave us a front row seat. For that awesome display of hard work, I am thankful to be the son of two city bus drivers. Once upon a time I was Richard and Susie's son, now they are Fedrick's parents. My best friends Richard (Duane), Randy, and Zach are also my brothers; we have done this thing called life together, each in our own way making footprints for our kids to follow. The best is yet to come.

To my wife, Yvetta, who tolerates me and my crazy life ideas. Two words, "Thank You." To my kids: Jordan, my son, the most courageous person I have ever known; Elan, my daughter, the truth teller and all-around superstar; and my baby Erin, the rock of our family, always remember that the world will give you only what you put in it. There will be hard times, disappointments, struggles, and pain, but you are the ones you need. Trust and take care of each other. I hope this book is a constant reminder that you can do anything you put your mind to, work for, and pray for... God Bless you my loves!

CONTENTS

Perseverance……………………………………………7

Love………………………………………………………25

Motivation……………………………………………38

Vision……………………………………………………57

Enthusiasm…………………………………………..72

Dedication……………………………………………86

Initiative………………………………………………99

Disruption…………………………………………..110

Finale………………………………………………….120

CADENCE OF LIFE

8 Traits For Winning In And Out Of The Classroom

CHAPTER 1

perseverance

NOUN

per·se·ver·ance

\ ˌpər-sə-ˈvir-ən(t)s \

: continued effort to do or achieve something despite difficulties, failure, or opposition

: the action or condition or an instance of persevering

"Whatever you fear most has no power – it is your fear that has the power. The thing itself cannot touch you. But if you allow your fear to seep into your mind and overtake your thoughts, it will rob you of your life."

- OPRAH WINFREY

Instead of beginning with a definition of perseverance, I will give you an illustration: a baby or toddler trying to learn how to walk. They don't just make it up in their minds that they want to walk and hop off the couch into a stride. Well, most of them don't. It is a process that involves learning how to stand with the aid of holding on to something, then learning how to stand on their own, after that transitioning to taking steps, possibly still holding on to a wall or a couch or a toy that encourages ambulatory aid, followed by walking with their arms outstretched until finally, they walk with a stride. The little one persevered through the process of learning. They didn't try, fall down and give up saying, "This is too hard." Little do they know, they are developing an attitude of perseverance to keep striving until they reach their goal that will serve them well into adulthood.

Perseverance is a key to success. It doesn't mean you will not fail; rather, you will not let the failure – or obstacle – stop you from trying. Slightly different than dedication, perseverance is the continued effort to achieve. This means you are doing the same action repeatedly or a series of actions to chip away at what is holding you back.

Despite how the end-result may look, even the greatest athletes, entrepreneurs, and public figures have suffered tremendous adversities that require perseverance to overcome them. They have emerged victorious after weathering the greatest of trials by sticking to their ideals and striving to reach their goals. We learn a great deal about ourselves once we realize the end goal is worth the effort. Even if we don't appreciate it at the time, persevering through each obstacle builds character.

My experience with this character trait began at a very young age. As I began speaking, I was diagnosed as a stutterer. I remember being in kindergarten, first, second, and third grade not fully able to get words out because of the stuttering issue. It was very difficult as a young kid trying to learn language and how to communicate without being fully able to. Stuttering at that age, people automatically think there is something wrong with your mind that you can't think or for some reason, you have fallen short, as in you don't have a normal IQ. Early on, I was placed in Exceptional Student Education (ESE) classes, even though there was nothing ever wrong with me mentally. I was just unable to communicate due to my speech impediment.

My mom, God bless her, went to every hospital in Miami-Dade, including children's hospitals. I was tested over and over. They ran so many tests on me as a young person, I thought that being familiar with doctors and nurses in sterile environments was the norm. Ultimately, I was diagnosed with a speech impediment, although the exact name escapes me now. However, speech impediments are fairly common and have nothing to do with neurological functions. According to the National Institute on Deafness and Other Communication Disorders (NIDCD), nearly 1 in 12 children ages 3–17 has had a disorder related to voice, speech, language, or swallowing. Boys are more likely than girls to have a communication disorder, and black children suffer more prevalently at a slightly elevated rate of 1-in-10.

So there I was, a young black male, with increased chances of having a speech impediment. Although some people inherit the disorder from a long line of stutterers, I did not. We did not have the genetic connection, but being a black boy did increase my odds of stuttering. This issue made elementary school quite difficult.

In first and second grades, I was placed in lower level academic classes. Thankfully, by third grade they found that I was fine mentally, so they removed me from ESE and placed me in general education classes.

We all know how cruel kids can be. The nicknames they made up for me were crazy. Two nicknames specifically come to mind, scratch record and tape recorder. Having my classmates pick on me forced me into a shy shell. For instance, when the teacher asked for class participation, I shied away. When teachers asked questions for the class to respond to, even if I knew the answer, I knew better than to raise my hand to attempt to say it. I feared the snickers, out right laughing, and whispers from my peers. The ridicule, to me, seemed worse than struggling to get the words out.

There were other teachers, however, who were not quite as understanding as to let me just not answer. They were under the impression that forcing me was the way to 'get it out' of me. They'd make me take a turn reading aloud to the class. I guess they thought it would help, but that didn't help me get over my impediment. It wasn't that I wanted to stutter, I didn't know how not to. I had not conditioned myself to breathe or enunciate and surely wasn't aware that there were ways to 'get it out.' I had not yet learned what words were more difficult to say like 'th' words or how to relax certain parts of my mouth to be able to say those words. It got to a point where reading aloud was the most mortifying experience ever.

Then came Ms. Lewis; she is one of the teachers I give a great deal of respect to. It seemed as though she really got it. She allowed me the privilege of walking to the board to write my answer instead of having me stand at my desk to answer like the other kids. Or she'd have me walk over to her desk to whisper my answer in her ear. She'd say, "I know you know the answer, come here." She did this in an attempt not to embarrass me.

Suffering through the embarrassment, there were many times when I thought, I'm not a normal person, I shouldn't be here. Looking at my classmates and friends, I did not fit into the scope of normalcy. My feelings of not being around weren't so prevalent that I contemplated suicide, but I definitely felt I would not be missed if I weren't around. It made me feel transparent and doubted my own intelligence sometimes. I knew I was as smart, if not more, than the rest of them; still I was too shy to speak out, or just too embarrassed. Some of my teachers thought I was being defiant and would angrily talk at me, "Hey, I'm talking to you!" I'd just look at them because I would rather be labeled as bad than to suffer unnecessary embarrassment when I could help it.

I am not the only person who was affected by my stuttering. My older brother used to get in so much trouble defending me. When he saw people pick on me, he'd step up. If he saw me crying at lunch time or after school, he was quick to ask, "Boy what's wrong with you?" All I had to do was point. My brother would charge in that direction. He didn't ask questions, he just started spouting off, "Don't mess with my brother!" I'm pretty sure in the time we were there, I caused my brother to have a rap sheet that could wrap around the school. Starting from elementary school all the way to high school, my brother was like *the man*. So when he told folks not to mess with me, they listened. I was always known as Rich's little brother. It seemed that nobody knew my name until he graduated high school; even then, I was still Rich's little brother.

My music teacher was instrumental, pun intended, in helping me cope with being picked on for stuttering. Early on, my speech therapists and linguistics teachers would pull me out of class to get tutoring for my speech impediment. Part of the therapy was learning how to control my breathing. I didn't quite get a grasp on this until my music teacher, Ms. Richardson, brought it on home for me. In essence, what brought me into music was my speech impediment.

My school had a huge chorus. It was arguably the best chorus in Miami-Dade County. Through her class, I found that when I sang, I didn't stutter. Eureka! It was like the clouds parted, bright rays of God's warm sunshine radiated through, and angels in heaven were singing along with me as I made this realization. Singing was the easiest thing ever! My speech pathologist's aim was to have me join a choir…any choir. I joined the school chorus and the church choir.

Ms. Richardson announced that we needed a lead singer for the class song that year which was, "We Are The World" by Michael Jackson and Lionel Richie. She whispered to me, "You are the best (hand)bell player we have, you can tinker on the piano, and you are so musically inclined. Why don't you audition for the lead?" I shook my head fervently, 'no!' "You sing really well," she added, "and you are a gifted musician."

As the story goes, I never actually auditioned. She called my mom saying she wanted me to sing for the sixth grade graduation and proceeded to give my mom all of the lines she wanted me to sing. My mom said, "Let's try it and see." My mom sat me down to have a conversation about it and I agreed to try it. Try.

What a monumental moment it was in my life. Me, a stutterer, standing on stage leading the largest elementary chorus in the county. People could not believe it. Everybody at the graduation was sitting on the edge of their seats in anticipation wondering how this boy, who had been stuttering all through school was going to sing lead on this song. It was like one of those awesome movie moments where the entire audience tears up. My principal, assistant principal, and a slew of teachers were in tears. It was absolutely crazy, especially for me. Even though I'd been practicing singing with no problem, and I'd had the revelation that I could sing without stuttering, standing behind that microphone was a different beast. I looked out into the sea of parents and students, I wasn't sure what was going to happen when I opened my mouth. I prayed that I'd be able to get it all out. Guess what? I didn't stutter, not even once. Talk about a huge win!

From that point on, I knew I had to stay close to music. It was like my saving grace. Music allowed me to be normal, to feel normal; but, most importantly to feel accepted. The other children couldn't pick on my musical ability because I was naturally good at it. Being 'normal' in music translated to the classrooms and playgrounds where I began to feel accepted.

Once I matriculated to middle school, there was a band, as well as a chorus. I never really liked to sing, so I opted to play in the band. From that point on, life was great. I developed my speech and enunciation so much that by high school, I became the captain of my speech and debate team. Going a step further, I was the co-captain on my collegiate speech and debate team. Looking at me now, I feel you'd be hard pressed to find someone who could have guessed that I had such a hard time speaking at all. On the contrary, those who knew me growing up found this version of me, the traveling public speaker and advocate, somewhat hard to believe.

How did I get past the stuttering? It was the power of prayer and persevering. When my mom told me to say prayers at night, I'd pray that God take my stuttering away because it kept people from liking me and wanting to be my friend. Being a stutterer made me an angry kid because nobody wanted to be around the kid with problems since that made me different. It seemed like I had a permanent attitude and I did because I felt ostracized from my peers and the world due to my speech. One day, I promised God if He allowed me to speak normally, I'd never stop talking.

Persevering came with sticking to speech therapy classes, practicing helpful techniques I was taught, and learning how to talk. It was an incredibly frustrating experience not to be able to just open my mouth and the words flow out as freely and easily as they did for the rest of the world. Until I got to a point of being comfortable speaking, I had to inch into that space by making the conscious effort to put my speech therapy lessons into practice each day. I still stuttered…people still laughed…I was still angry…the cycle continued. I kept continuing the action of chipping away at the obstacle until I was able to speak with more fluidity.

Now, I travel the country as an advocate for students to receive equal educational resources. However, the taunting and ridicule of my childhood are never far behind me. I have to persevere through the feelings of nervousness each time I step up to microphones speaking to crowds of thousands, pushing the sounds of students snickering behind me out of my mind. There is no cure for stuttering, either you outgrow it or you learn to control it through breathing and enunciating techniques. For me, I was fortunate enough to master controlling it. I often share this story of childhood heartache and conquering to empower others. We all have obstacles to overcome; there are differences each one of us possesses that we must persevere through. It's so easy to look at what makes us unique and view it as a hindrance. In your experience, it may very well be.

Instead of viewing hindrances as obstacles, we should view them as opportunities; opportunities to shine and find where our strengths lie. We have to love the skin we are in. I stress this to kids everywhere I go. Embrace who you are, the way you wear your hair, the clothes you have. Not only do you have to learn to cope with your lot in life, whatever that may be, but you also have to learn to love it. If you can't accept and love who you are, shortcomings and all, how can you expect to love someone else? We all have some cross to bear. You may not know what someone else's cross is, but trust me, there's something. Don't think your cross is bigger than anybody else's; it's just different.

There are a few affirmative perseverance statements you can apply to your daily life:
- I believe in myself.
- I know what goals I want to accomplish.
- Change does not frighten me.
- I know my limitations.
- I have great friends and family who support me striving for my goals.
- I bounce back from disappointments.
- I am able to complete projects.
- Fear does not control me.

When you set out to achieve a task, remember your motivation (see Chapter 3). As an educator, you have a heart for children and their futures. Let that fuel the fire you need to persevere through downfalls and power over obstacles. You will suffer through challenging days where the kids seem impossible to wrangle under control, or you will be pumped to receive a nomination for an award only to be let down when you are not selected.

The minute you want to give up is the precise time not to. Understand that perseverance is not only for you, but for your students as well. They will emulate what they see you model. Encourage them to understand that mistakes are how we learn. You make mistakes, then keep working until you find a way that yields a favorable result. I truly feel that this is one of the most critical skills we, as educators, can model and pass forward to our students.

You may find it easy to encourage pupils and co-workers to persevere through their mistakes, while doing the same for yourself could be a bitter pill to swallow. It is easy to see that struggling creates opportunities for growth in the lives of others; however, viewing your own life through the same lens leaves you frustrated and overwhelmed.

Helping your students cultivate attitudes of perseverance through you-can-do-it teaching strategies will help them focus on elements of achievement. This will only strengthen them down the road. For instance, many times, youngsters will come up against a certain task that they feel unable to effectively complete. In my specialty, let's say a student was challenged in band practice counting rhythms or beats. Over time, the student would grow frustrated and fall behind their peers upholding this standard. Rather than endure years of opposition struggling to keep the beat, the student would more than likely end up withdrawing from band. Whereas, if I employ techniques such as meeting with the student after rehearsal or pairing them with a student who excels at counting rhythms, the student will learn to persevere. Not only am I helping to develop leadership in one student, but at the same time using peer pressure to teach the other student to persevere.

Keep moving, keep persevering. Each goal you set for yourself will not be easy and will test your endurance. After all, the purpose of setting goals is to improve. Some goals will be easily attainable, while others will require a great deal of perseverance to get through. If you know you will need additional support, enlist the help of supportive friends and family. Asking them to be your accountability partners will help ensure your success. Encourage your students to do the same.

What are a few affirmative perseverance statements you can specify to your life?

CHAPTER 2

love

NOUN

love

\ ˈləv \

: affection based on admiration, benevolence, or common interests

: the object of attachment, devotion, or admiration

"Love is not only something you feel, it is something you do."

- DAVID WILKERSON

Growing up, you experience a myriad of emotions as you go from being a baby, where the world seems to revolve around you…to entering school, where social groups begin to form…to middle and high school where you are not only trying to put your stamp of individuality on life, but also find out what it's all about anyway.

Searching for a meaning or purpose in life is not something most of us intentionally seek until we are well into adulthood. At some point you realize all of the headaches, irritations of the day, and emotions you go through must serve a purpose. It makes no sense to be constantly confused or inconvenienced for no reason. But really, until we believe that there is a higher purpose, we are merely floating along with the tide.

That higher purpose is finding something or someone we love. Love, not to be confused with passion, is one of the things that makes every*thing* matter. Love inspires. Love creates. Love perseveres. Love makes it all worthwhile. Love leads you to find your 'why.' Deep feelings of enthusiasm and devotion surround you anytime you are in the presence of what you love. It's a wonderful, glorious feeling that can have you jumping from the rafters or swirling around like the renowned scene in 'The Sound of Music' when Julie Andrews flails her arms circling around on the rolling hills of Salzburg.

Some of us love out of duty, then there are those of us who love with purpose. Are you confused about the difference? Loving for duty is a steady, calm appreciation. Loving with purpose is an energized, excited love. That is the love that coaxes you to keep trying when you fail, or to put your best foot forward, or act a certain way when nobody is looking.

That is how I feel about music. Music gives me a sense of purpose, an excitement that I feel in my bones. I developed this love of music at an early age when many of my peers' enjoyment of music only went as deep as the catchy hooks or melodies from popular tunes we heard our parents blasting on Saturday mornings while cleaning up. I felt intricacies of cadences and melodies way down deep. I knew music was going to play a major role in my life. Not only had I found something I was great at, but it was something I enjoyed. And I'm not talking great like acts who audition on shows such as American Idol because they want to take their shower singing to the next level or their parents told them they could sing. I'm talking real, God-given talent where in many instances my abilities superseded my own expectations. I don't say this to brag, but my love for music has carved a way for me to be the man I am today. It came about in an interesting way.

During my freshman year in high school, there was a young lady who was a year ahead of me. As a 10th grader, she was arguably the most serious musician we had in our high school band. At that point, I knew music was going to be one of the great loves of my life. I had a deep desire to expound upon the role that music played in my life beyond the way many of my friends saw it. Most of my peers' appreciation for music encompassed popular songs on the radio and whatever was blasting from boom boxes or box Chevys cruising down the street. What I learned from my bandmate was that she had an undeniable hunger for music and learning music that drove her to practice all the time. She was active in music competitions going up against others who also had the same fervent type of love and rivalry for supremacy. She took on a seriousness that, up until that point, I had never really seen. It didn't matter that we were kids from the hood who grew up with less than what other kids had.

Initially, I felt like my fondness for her was due to how attractive she was, or that she was a nice girl with a genuinely good heart. Ultimately, I realized that fondness was more of an admiration. Seeing the pride she took in her craft, wanting to be the best flutist she could be. I admired her love for striving for superiority, wanting to improve even after others told her she was the best, striving for greatness. She practiced and practiced, honing her skill. Her love of purpose, to me, was profound.

It took me years to truly comprehend what a phenomenal impact she had on me by simply watching her do what she was doing. She led by example like my parents, not by telling or teaching her bandmates, but by doing. As the David Wilkerson quote started the chapter, "Love is not only something you feel, it is something you do."

We all witnessed her working to be a better version of herself championing. The revelation brought such a deeper meaning to the old adage, "Actions speak louder than words." The reason this section is important to me is to shed light on how leading by example can make an impact on the lives of others. Dedicating time and effort to those things that we know we should do or enjoy doing are what give us purpose. The reflection taught me that we often influence others through our love of what we were doing who we don't even know are watching.

While I am friends with this young lady to this day, we don't see or speak to one another often; however, the reflections of us in the band room at Miami Jackson High School still speak to me. During that critical time in my life where I could have easily deviated onto the wrong path or simply given up, she actively taught me that the heights I aspired to reach required an elevated level of discipline. At the same time, she showed me how love resonates through actions when moving in your purpose regardless of what was going on around me. In times of frustration or peril, I would glance over at her and wind up doing the right thing, because she was doing the right thing. In this way, her love for improving her musical prowess created a domino effect if you will.

Think for a minute what a profound effect she had on me at that young age. What if I did give up?

What if I was so frustrated with playing that I stopped? What if I didn't persevere? Where would I be today? Would I have ever gone to college on a scholarship? Would I have gotten a college degree? Would I have pressed forward to make a sizable enough impression to ultimately become Teacher of the Year for Miami-Dade County? Would I have left the classroom to be an advocate for disenfranchised students around the state?

When she put her lips to that flute, my life's course being on the straight and narrow was not a part of her mission. She taught me that if you know what you're looking for and how to find it, you can change the world. Watching her lead by example as my peer gave me 'permission' to strive to be a better, more passionate version of myself when putting effort into something I loved.

I challenge you to let love lead you. Allow yourself to be free to love your purpose and dwell on enriching the lives of others through your craft and ingenuity. After all, music is meant to be shared. You don't have to be like anyone else to be great. I didn't have to play the flute like my bandmate, but I did follow in the footprints that she set forth with continuous practice. I took part in competitions and

Cadence of Life 33

worked hard as to extend my knowledge so I could manipulate my instrument to a level of excellency. You will be amazed how much joy is paralleled with the power, engagement, and fun that accompanies putting your all into something. Love for your 'why' makes the work no longer feel like work. You can help to heal students, co-workers, and yourself; strengthen their belief in themselves, as well as yourself; you can also reignite the fire in them as they watch you act in your own awesomeness.

As you walk through this life striving to grasp your full potential, keep a vision ahead of you that you have yet to realize. Never forget that while you are coming into a better version of yourself, you are also stimulating and encouraging others along the way with the love they see exhibiting from you.

Find ways to fall back in-love with teaching. Seek out opportunities to point out positivity in the classroom. This can easily be accomplished by celebrating the students' successes. If you have a student who really gets a new concept, applaud that. On the contrary, if it seems a student is having difficulty getting the new concept and finally succeeds, celebrate that. Let them revel in learning something new and see your joy because you love sharing your purpose.

If a student makes a witty comment that incites a roar of laughter, let it be. Enjoy the comic relief. Yes, education is serious business; but that doesn't mean you have to take it so seriously. If the students see you are having fun, guess what? They will have fun too!

Work side-by-side with colleagues to form alliances in planning lessons together. Introduce contests to the students to get them as motivated to learn as you are to teach. If you see an area where a fellow co-worker can improve, pull them aside to lend them a few nuggets of wisdom from your expertise. And do so to help make their experience a more well-rounded one, not expecting anything in return.

Whatever your occupation, find ways to genuinely love what you do. Maintain a positive mindset by avoiding harmful conversations about your profession, saying things that highlight the not-so-exciting aspects of teaching.

If you are reading this book, you believe teaching is your purpose. You know how tremendous your impact is to future generations and appreciate your position to do so.

What are a few ways to cultivate love of your purpose?

Practice self-love. I know, I know, it sounds cliché. 'Self-love' is one of the hot button phrases in recent years due to increasing suicides, suicide attempts, and technology causing an increased lack of personal interaction even though we seem to be more easily connected. You need a good night's sleep to feel refreshed, healthy food and exercise to rejuvenate the body, and hobbies to reinvigorate the soul. Meet up with friends for laughs and keep a positive mindset. Practicing self-love outside of the classroom will show inside the classroom.

Connect with your inner self. You are more than a title; yet, that is how many of us define ourselves. Your true identity is deeper than changing circumstances in your life. Connect with your inner being through prayer, meditation, journaling, or intentional alone time.

If you find yourself challenged during the day, steal away a few moments to inhale and exhale deeply.

This will help you to re-center yourself allowing you to approach teaching with a renewed mental shift.

Don't let failure win. If you truly love doing something, this goes without saying. You will want to take a break, but you won't want to give up. Nor should you. Frustration will come, but free yourself enough to let love nudge you back in the right direction.

Own your authenticity. You are who you are. We often pain ourselves by trying to stifle our creativity and the 'it' that makes us different. Let your burning desires and dreams fuel you. Being your authentic self is one of the most empowering feelings in the world!

Describe an experience that has led you to love what you do.

CHAPTER 3

motivation

NOUN

mo·ti·va·tion

\ ˌmō-tə-ˈvā-shən \

: the act or process of motivating

: a motivating force, stimulus, or influence

Cadence of Life

"Start where you are, use what you have, do what you can."

- ARTHUR ASHE

According to Merriam-Webster, motivation is defined as a motivating force, stimulus, or influence. The root word, motive, speaks to our desires, wants, or needs. Motivation is a stimulus that drives us to set in motion a series of actions that will help us to reach our goals. Actions, as we know, are not passive. This means you are intentionally taking the steps necessary to see something to fruition or earn something you yearn for.

Motivating forces come in all shapes and sizes. The carrot dangling in front of the donkey can be a particular job, a partner, a new house, or an intangible feeling such as happiness. For most, we have motivators that are somehow related to money. Well, doesn't it seem to always circle back around to money in one form or another? Earning enough money to pay bills, support your family, go on vacation, or impress others.

Once you have consciously or subconsciously identified your motivator, that is what keeps you pushing forward. We set goals all of the time; setting them is the easy part. Following through with the actions necessary to reach those goals are where we fall short. Take the New Year for example. It has been estimated that as many as 93% of Americans make New Year's Resolutions! Yet, as few as 8% are motivated enough to keep those resolutions. Maintaining motivation is not something that befalls us naturally; it is developed over time. What makes maintaining motivation so challenging is most of the goals we set are unrealistically attainable. So what ends up happening is we fall short, become frustrated and burned out, or suffer from waning willpower.

This brings me back to the dangling carrot...your reason. What is your motivating push to succeed? Mine was very close to home, my grandmother. Grandmother was born and raised in rural Georgia mostly between Dublin and Albany. She'd only received a third grade education, while my grandfather had a sixth grade education. Together, they had 11 children. They migrated down to Miami because my grandfather got a job with the railroads way back when. He was a part of the influx of black railroad construction workers Standard Oil and FEC railroad tycoon Henry Flagler brought down to modernize the existing network to accommodate heavier loads and more traffic of the expansive, luxurious hotels he was building up and down Florida's East Coast.

Having such a limited education, grandmother could barely read. As a matter of fact, she marked her signature with an 'x'. If you don't know, whenever a legal document required signature by someone who was illiterate or disabled, they would simply write an 'x' in lieu of their name. I am unsure of how the authentication process worked if the 'x' was challenged, since many signatures were just the single letter, however, it worked. My grandmother signing her name that way meant she could not read or write.

Regardless of the book knowledge she may have lacked, she was very wise. It's hard to imagine how even without ever being able to read, she was able to view the world with such a unique perspective that to this day, I still have not ever met anyone quite like her.

She understood the value of education, but nobody in my direct genealogy had gone to college. There was nothing to make me think that I could ever go to college or that I was even college material. Many of my extended family, cousins, aunts, and uncles didn't even graduate high school. My mom was the youngest of the bunch. Everybody poured into her. You have to think, as the baby of 11, they all took care of her. The fact that she was so smart helped her case. They all wanted her to graduate high school.

When my brothers and I were coming up, my mother often referenced the importance of education. She shared with us that while growing up, she would read to my grandmother to let her know what was going on in the world. They both understood the importance of reading the newspaper, especially the black newspaper. Even beyond that, my mother became very fluid in her literacy with this practice.

My grandmother also harped on the significance of a good day's work. She'd say, "You can do all of that college stuff, but make sure you get a job so you can make some money." With non-existent exposure to collegiate life, she did not fully comprehend that a successful grind at college would set me up for more than just 'a job.' By high school, I knew being a college graduate was something I saw in my future. All of the signs were there. Great encouragement from my teachers, excellent report cards and loving the track I was on. At the same token, I was close to my grandmother. I knew she would never talk me out of a dream that could do nothing but benefit me. Yet, constant conversations had her probing me about what kind of job I was going to get, whether or not I was learning to read, and if I was learning basic math functions. I recall being a fourth grader and my grandmother asking me if I could read. To me it was almost comical to be hitting double digits at 10-years-old and asked if I could read. From kindergarten to my freshmen year in college, she asked, "Fed, can you read all those books?" Part of me believes that she was in awe that what she saw as jumbled letters on paper formed words that told me stories or taught me the ways of the world.

Aside from that, my grandmother loved music. Now, she couldn't play an instrument nor could she sing, but her love for music was genuine and infectious. She'd constantly ask if we knew of any famous musicians coming to town or if we knew of any concerts coming up. She'd try to chip in to get tickets giving us some of the rolled up coins from her closet. We used to wheel her around to concerts, getting good seats in the handicap section because she wanted to be there! She was not playing! There was an annual Budweiser Superfest Concert series that came to the city. The biggest names came to the fest each year such as Luther Vandross, Whitney

Houston, and Patti LaBelle. By the time she saw Luther perform, she was around 80-years-old.

This was a far cry from the life she'd known growing up. She had a hard life of picking peanuts in the fields under the blistering South Georgia sun. She never had a job the way we have come to think of jobs today, it was all manual labor type of work, while raising her brood of children. I was blessed enough to get to see her in her older age. Yes, she got around on a walker for just about my whole life from what I can remember. She was a little heavy, with big eyes, thick glasses, and the prettiest Gabrielle Union shade of brown skin. As we wheeled her around to events like Superfest, she'd flash that complete set of dentures at us with the quickness. It made me happy to see her happy and to know that we had something in common: our love for music.

When it was time for me to go to college, she pulled me to the side and said, "If you're gonna go to that schoolhouse, you better do good. I want you to get whatever they're gonna give you because I heard on the TV that you can get a really good job." Then she walked me into her room and opened the closet. For years and years, she'd been rolling up change and stacking it in her closet. She gave me half of the small fortune she'd amassed. Honestly, it wasn't much. At the end of the day it was a bunch of pennies rolled up, but to her, she may as well have given me her house or her last will and testament. There was so much thought and love behind that gesture, it certainly was not lost on me. Everybody was telling her 'Fedrick is going away to school…he's going to a big college – Bethune-Cookman, a very small, private school especially back then…it's sooo far away – Daytona Beach was only four hours in a car…he's not going to be able to come home.' It was a really big deal for me to go away to college because nobody else had gone.

My high school band director, Mr. McKenzie believed in me also. I can still hear him telling me, "You're a little different than the rest of these kids." He tried his best to keep my nose clean. Being a snappy little knucklehead, I'd get into fights at the school. Mr. McKenzie would pull me into his office and question, "What are you doing, man? You're going to throw your whole life away for some kid who stepped on your shoe!" He really made a point to connect with me, because he cared and nurtured me, our relationship forged a tight bond.

There was such a sense of pride from my family when I went off to college. Even my hood cousins knew about FAMU (Florida A&M University) and BCU; they were excited to ask questions about how I got into the school. There were a wide range of occupations in my family, but we couldn't trace anybody who had gone to college on my mother's side. Going to college was a tremendous feat for me. My family acknowledged this milestone. It seemed as though I sprouted wings and was promoted to an angel. You would think this put a lot of pressure on me, but it was quite the opposite. Since there was no one for them to really compare me to, there was no expectation like in born-and-bred college families you know, where kids are not only expected to go away to college, but earn degrees, and possibly go back for graduate degrees.

Instead of placing a burden to succeed on me, I received support from them. It was more like, "Go do your thing whatever that is. Go get the experience and if it works out for you, you're alright with us. Even if it doesn't, you're still good." With my trunk and two suitcases, my parents dropped me off at Bethune-Cookman. I cried and they cried; I'm not even a crier. For me to cry was the equivalent of my whole world caving in on me, but that day was unlike any other. When my parents got ready to leave me, I was thinking, *What in the heck am I doing?* This was the furthest I was going to be away from my family. Back home, my whole family lived within 20 blocks of each other. And when I say whole family, we're talking uncles, aunts, and cousins, everybody!

My first year in college after finishing band camp and a few weeks after school started, I went home for the weekend. Coincidentally, we didn't have a game, so it was the perfect time for my first trip home which was after about a month and a half. I was ecstatic to see my family, especially my grandmother. She held a special place in my heart. It didn't matter how many children and grandchildren she had, she and I had a special bond. Everybody feels like they are the matriarch's favorite. I knew I truly was.

Upon arriving in town, I went to my grandmother's apartment in the projects. All her life, she'd lived in public housing. I spent the night Friday and stayed over there half of Saturday. As I was getting ready to leave, I went in her room to let her know. As soon as the words escaped my mouth, she went into cardiac arrest and died in my arms. My mom and a few of my younger cousins were there. My mom lost it, so did my cousins. I was the only one who could keep it together. I dialed 9-1-1 and held my grandmother in my arms at the same time. The paramedics didn't pronounce her dead there, but she was already gone.

Her passing away really hurt me. She never got to see me realize my dream of becoming a college graduate. She knew it was important for me to go; I knew it was important for me to go and thrive. We both knew it was going to transcend our family name to go from generational poverty to something that we could all believe in. I would be able to usher in a new era of greatness and set higher expectations.

My grandmother is where I got a significant part of my drive from. Even in her death, she motivated me to make it right. I wanted to be the one to build our family name. I didn't want to have our family poor and struggling for generations to come. I knew there was a better way and the fact that she believed in me after all those years of telling me to grow up and get a job, showed me her unrelenting support.

Suffering such a blow to my system, I almost didn't go back to college. It kind of felt like there was no point anymore. Here it was, my heart, my motivation had passed away. One of the band instructors, James Poitier, who still works with the band to this day said, "If you don't get yourself together and get your butt in this school, everything you did to get here is going to be all for naught." I told him I didn't know how I was going to do it. Everything in me was gone. I was still shuffling around Miami two weeks later because I couldn't bring myself to go back to school. It was around this time that I found not one, but two new sources of motivation. One had been there all along, I just didn't know it.

I realized that being a college student made me proud. Being a Marching Wildcat gave me something else to be proud about. In fact, the only reason I even knew Mr. Poitier, Mr. P. as he is respectfully called, was because of the band. And I felt like a superhero in my band uniform. When the band played in Miami for Battles of the Band or for games, I was like the king of my block. I mean 'The King'…for many years going forward. It all started the first time my home town saw me in that Marching Wildcats uniform.

Prior to me going away to school, I had only seen the band one time. Well, Bethune-Cookman that is. I was more familiar with FAMU's band because they traveled down to Miami all the time. Back in those days, Bethune-Cookman didn't travel down to Miami very much. I saw them come to Miami one time, which I believe was my junior year in high school. By that time, I was already a hot shot saxophone player. Mr. P. graduated from the same high school that I was attending, Miami Jackson High. So when he let me know he came from the same place I did, seeing him walk around in his BCU blazer as one of the band directors made the possibility real for me. He came from Liberty City just like me. I was able to see a walking, living, breathing manifestation of what before seemed like a dream that was not an attainable goal. That day was the day I chose BCU as the next stop on my educational journey. I can remember vividly thinking, *This cat came from the hood and he's the band director?* That made an impression on me to want to do more. At the time, I didn't know exactly what that more was, I just knew I couldn't excel where I was. I liked the uniforms, the music, and now I had an additional source of motivation in the wake of my grandmother's passing. Mr. P. was someone I did not want to disappoint.

Remember when I said one of the sources of my motivation had been around me the whole time? I was talking about my peeps from the neighborhood. Once my cousins and friends found out I was smarter than the average kid, they came with the pressure, "Yo, you gotta do this college thing man." Even some of the street pharmacists I knew actually began giving me money to encourage me to stay off the streets. They saw something in me before I saw it in myself. They saw hope, they saw promise, they saw a future and didn't want me to succumb to the temptations of watching them make quick, fast money. They would even push me away. If they saw me walk up on them in or around the hood, they'd tell me, "Naw Fed. Get from 'round here!"

On breaks from college, those same kids from high school who greased my palms and pushed me away continued to do the same. They wouldn't let me hang out with them on the street corner or at the park. "You doin' good bruh, keep it up," they'd say. They'd dap me up with a couple 20's or 100's and send me on my way. Once they saw that I went away to college and persevered instead of dropping out and coming back home, they encouraged me by keeping me away from trouble. It was as if no one wanted to be responsible for my downfall, which I greatly appreciate. It also gave me the desire to drive through to succeed. I wanted to do well for the memory of my grandmother, but I also had people who were still alive who wanted to bear witness that I actually did it!

You know what? I did not disappoint them! I walked across the stage at Bethune-Cookman as the first person in my family to graduate college.

Both of the motivators I described were extrinsic: my grandmother and my community. We will give an honorable mention to Mr. P. who gave his two cents to bring me back to BCU after my grandmother passed away.

Motivating students can be a difficult task, but the rewards of watching them succeed are great. Instructing a class full of motivated learners is a great experience for you as their teacher, as well as for them. When you can take any one of the boring, mundane subjects that kids dread and make it fascinating, that creates a motivated learner. Breathing life into the words on the page to help them understand how this information will one day be relevant to their lives will make them want to keep learning. Furthermore, in mastering the tests and assignments, they gain a sense of accomplishment that will motivate them to attack other subjects and areas of their lives with similar zest.

The classroom environment can be very demanding. Let's be honest, students don't really see us as humans, especially if our demeanor always comes across as overly serious. Usually, we spend our class periods trying to get students to calm down, focus on the lesson, and be quiet. Our faces are stern and conduct, strict. We open up a book and teach or spend the period writing on the board. Now, what about that encourages motivated learning?

Try smiling, asking the students how their days are going, then actually listen for their response. Bust up your routine of doing things 'by the book' which will freshen the environment. Think outside of the box instead of rigidly standing at the front of the class talking *at* your students, walk around and turn the lesson into more of a conversation with them. Perhaps take a walk on the wild side by divvying up the syllabus to let each child model teaching a section.

Joel Osteen, prominent televangelist in Houston, Texas begins each one of his sermons with a joke. Doing this breaks down stiff walls of nervousness or apprehension. Try doing the same in your classroom. Adding a more human element to yourself will make your students feel more relaxed and encourages responses from them because you seem more approachable. This will motivate them not to want to disappoint you. They will strive to make you proud, each one of them having a unique connection with you.

A bonus to putting your motivation to teach on display is the behavior in the room should improve. They won't be so bored and easily distracted if you are engaging them with unique teaching strategies.

It is not a far-fetched thought process that an exceptional teacher can change a child's life. Think of someone who motivated you and how they changed your life for the better. Now pay it forward.

Name a person who has motivated you in the past.

_____

How did they motivate you?

_____
_____
_____

Do you think you would have been successful without them?

_____
_____

Why or why not?

_____
_____

What is another source of motivation in the present day picture of your life? Why?

_____
_____
_____

CHAPTER 4

vision

NOUN

vi·sion

\ ˈvi-zhən \

: the act or power of imagination

: mode of seeing or conceiving

: unusual discernment or foresight

"The only thing worse than being blind is having sight but no vision."

- Helen Keller

Cadence of Life 59

You will often hear that having a vision for your life is critical. Proverbs 29:18 (KJV) says, "Where there is no vision the people perish." Just hearing the term, 'have a vision for your life' seems a bit generic.

What exactly is a vision? A vision is a bigger picture. It is an image of success that you hold in your head, or heart, giving you something to strive toward. Your vision illustrates what you want to be known for, who you want to be, and what you want to build. Most of us will say we want to build a legacy; but what kind of legacy?

Vision isn't the perseverance to overcome obstacles, or the right attitude about tackling tasks, or even the initiative to begin. Vision isn't planning the 'how to achieve' or the motivation, which is your why. Vision is the what. What do you want to accomplish? What do you see yourself doing? What do you want your children's children to know about you?

The legacy I was looking to leave, at first, did not begin much different from the one I'd been given. I was born into a life of poverty in the inner city. I often discuss generational poverty because my grandmother lived in the projects her entire life.

Most of my elementary school years were spent living in the projects. My dad was a city bus driver who said he'd rather for us to struggle than for my mom to work. My father was very old fashioned in his beliefs that a woman should be taken care of so she could take care of the home. At the time, there were three of us, my youngest brother came much later. Dad was devoted to being the provider of the home no matter what he had to do. I remember a time when my dad left the house at four in the morning to go to work, came home around the time we arrived from school, then was right back out of the door in a different uniform. He worked double shifts for years because he was adamant about my mom being home to raise their sons.

With all of the love between my parents, they had me and two of my brothers all within four years, so the struggle of providing coupled with my dad's mindset presented quite a challenge. That is how we ended up in public housing. As you can imagine, if you don't have first-hand knowledge of living in the projects yourself, we were exposed to all sorts of things. For example, I've seen people get shot in the park, along with a slew of other unmentionables. One of my best friends' brothers led a carjacking ring in the inner-city. They used a part of our housing project to strip the cars and put them on bricks. The crazy part about it is, we all knew what type of operation it was. When we saw a new car come in, we knew that car was only going to be there looking all nice and pretty for about another 30 minutes because it was going to be sitting on bricks momentarily.

My brother, Rich, was as tough as they came. He wasn't bad, but he was a no nonsense person. He could fight and would 'throw them bows' as Ludacris said, if he needed to. Homeboy was zero talk, all action. While I always felt I was protected, I also felt the pressure of a tough boy image to uphold. My brother coming before me molded me into a no nonsense person. I would tell people quickly, "I've already seen more than anybody can put me through."

Life was hard. Can you fathom living in the beautiful, tropical metropolis of Miami…only not on the beachside…but in a house in the inner city with no air condition? My parents bought a window air condition unit and placed it in the living room.

That room felt amazing leaving the rest of the house to feel like an inferno. We didn't have a washer and dryer in the house. We had to walk to the wash house four blocks away lugging baskets or pillowcases overflowing with clothes.

And if that wasn't enough, we moved around a lot. Literally moving every year. One of the caveats of public housing that I would come to learn later was the government didn't want you making your space into a home. The housing was cheap, but we were relocated every nine months or so even though it was within the same 15 blocks. The approach now is a bit different, where Section 8 allows you to afford to rent a home with the hope that you will take pride in it and integrate yourself into becoming a part of the community. The city is concerned about the cosmetic effect projects had with the surrounding businesses. That wasn't the case when I was growing up.

Being in an environment with less than desirable activity flying around taught me many things, how to be tough, how to struggle, but not how to have vision. Racial dignity was real, but only mattered inside the boundaries of your own community.

My mom only began to work during my sophomore year in high school because I made it clear that going to college was a dream of mine. She'd heard that going to college was expensive and of course, they didn't have any type of college fund or money saved up for us. Two pivotal things happened during this timeframe that gave and shaped my vision. Being in the band and seeing the BCU band come to Miami and a wildly popular TV show, *A Different World,* that rose to prominence during those years made me feel like I could go to college and be successful in a career. That world was so different than the one in which I grew up. I was looking for a Hillman! If I could have found a college named Hillman, I would have applied in a heartbeat just because of the name alone!

My college experience changed my life, it is the reason I am who I am today. Going to Bethune-Cookman was the first time I saw a community of home owners who were black. I'd never seen a community flourishing with entrepreneurs, private practices, and academia scholars. Everybody in my family lived in the projects, worked the streets, and worked hard, mostly manual jobs.

I heard the professors referred to as doctors left and right. I was trying to make the correlation between how all of my professors delivered babies or helped sick kids and still managed to teach at the university. Coming from my background, the only doctors I knew of were the ones who delivered babies or those who I saw when I was sick. I kept saying to myself, *All of these people must be really smart if they also went to medical school.*

This whole new world opened up for me to see occupations and upstanding members of the community to emulate. I remember going to Dr. Powell's house thinking, *Man! This guy lives in a mansion.* Dr. Powell was also a member of the band staff with Mr. P. The more engrained I became in the community, the more impressed I was as people displayed their intelligence and accomplishments, not in a braggadocios way, but in just going about their day-to-day lives type of way. I saw levels of success that I had not ever been exposed to, beyond *A Different World*, to be able to dream about.

In addition, the people I was seeing didn't look like they were hurting the way those in my home environment did. The people who had been around me while I was growing up who were gainfully employed worked hard jobs. They were always tired and hurting; dirty from work and had to jump straight in the shower when they got home. That remembrance was a far cry from the spritely steps I saw from professionals wearing suits and flowy dresses all dolled up, high-tailing it around campus. I thought, *This is awesome! This is how I want to live.*

Then when I looked at the students, it seemed that we all were on the same playing field. We were all broke; nobody had anything, but we wanted to have something, we wanted to be somebody. Classmates would say, "I want to be an architect. I want to be an engineer. I want to start a family business." What was so invigorating was that I'd never had those types of conversations before. I had never been around people who sought to make moves that would position them and future generations for greatness. I hadn't been around people my age who, not only believed that there was a better way of living, but also put plans into action to achieve the way of living they desired.

At Bethune-Cookman, I was living in a positively altered reality. In my head, I was the Dwayne Wayne, dark-skinned, skinny boy with glasses. He even wore a high top fade on his long, slim head like I did. That show really inspired me.

Being in this new environment jolted me in a good way. It took me away from the bubble of struggle and poverty that I was used to, placing me in a new atmosphere that facilitated growth, a mental stretch that propelled me to see that possibilities were endless. It was such an awesome feeling to know I could have one of the careers that I saw on TV. A vision had evolved for me; a new, fresh approach to life in a way that wouldn't wear me down or keep me down.

Having a vision for what you want is equally as important as how you plan to obtain it. When you feel stuck in a rut, reimagining your vision will help you get moving on the right track. Thinking about why you got into education in the first place is a great place to start. Hopefully, you came into this field with purpose and a goal to pour into our youngsters.

Recall what the vision of you being in the classroom looked like before you stepped foot into the classroom. Are you presently there? Does your day-to-day look the way you envisioned it? If it does, great! Think of ways to grow as an educator to make a more substantial impact. If it doesn't, Why not? What can you do to change where you are?

We all come into periods where we feel stagnant in our personal lives, as well as our professional lives. This is where having a vision comes into play. To be honest, sometimes being burned out can lead you to a place where you are not able to cultivate a vision of your own. In that space, it is ok to borrow someone else's vision. What do I mean by that? Two words: teachers' conferences.

Conferences and conventions are incredible ways to see what is new in the field. You will meet teachers across a far-reaching area and come into contact with vendors from around the country enlightening you with knowledge of what's out there in your area of expertise. These encounters will reignite the imagery in your vision. You will come into fresh ways to engage your students and introduce material in an exciting way. As your students respond positively to the new types of interaction you introduce, you will be further encouraged to continue with the trend. Your vision of being an unforgettable instructor will be bursting with innovative teaching techniques and exercises.

Already out of the classroom? You should have a vision for leading. As an administrator or working in corporate office, you can still have visions for the direction in which your career goes. Do you want to move up the ladder? What does that look like? Would you like to transition to a new position? How do you get there? Would you like to go to another school district? How can you put your best foot forward? You have to go to work every day, so why not have a vision for a more exciting, dedicated, and helpful version of that job?

You have the ability to truly transform the way you view your profession by thinking boldly and daring yourself to dream. Reorganize your classroom; reconfigure your thoughts; re-envision your career and re-evaluate your program of deliverance annually to see if your input equals your output.

If you are stuck as to how you can find your vision for your personal life, follow these tips.

Identify what priorities to you. There is no right or wrong answer to this statement. We are all different.

Whether reaching an ideal weight takes precedence, starting a family or excelling in your career, pinpoint the things that mean the most to you.

***Divide what matters into categories*:**
- Health
- Ability
- Relationships
- Contentment
- Experiences
- Wealth
- Accomplishments

Set goals. Goals are obviously meant to be attainable, but usually the goals we set for ourselves are far-reaching. Develop short and long-term goals for each category which will give you something to strive toward. This will lead to fulfillment and happiness.

Set the vision. Find a picture of what you want. Computer screens, phone lock screens, and vision boards are great places to put picturesque representations for what you want. This will keep the images fresh and give you gentle nudges to keep working in the right direction.

Positive affirmations. Whatever you aspire to do, the vision begins in your mind. Speak positive 'I am' statements that affirm you will see your visions manifest.

- I am…a successful entrepreneur.
- I am…in a loving, happy relationship.
- I am…mentally healthy and strong.
- I am…in alignment with God's purpose for my life.
- I am…a New York Times Bestselling author.
- I am…the owner of a Maserati Quattroporte.
- I am…financially free to travel as I please.

Find or create the vision you want for your life. Don't stop until you have achieved it.

What was your career vision five years ago?

_____
_____
_____

Have you achieved that vision?

_____

Why or why not?

_____

What is your current vision for your career?

_____
_____
_____
_____

Name an accountability partner who can help you achieve this vision.

_____

CHAPTER 5

enthusiasm

NOUN

en·thu·si·asm

\ in-ˈthü-zē-ˌa-zəm \

: something inspiring zeal or fervor

: strong excitement of feeling

"Nothing great was ever achieved without enthusiasm."

- RALPH WALDO EMERSON

Enthusiasm, in a word, is bottled up excitement. It was derived from the Greek word, *enthousiasmos*, meaning to be inspired or possessed by a divine being. Enthusiasm is a tool that drives momentum and feelings of happiness, while inciting positive energy.

Standing in front of a classroom, it's easy to begin the school year as full of energy as the room is full of students. It is all about beginning something new. No matter where you are in your journey of life, just the thought alone of starting something new brings with it a sense of nervous excitement. Think about the hype around New Year celebrations, the wildly popular countdowns, and going into new seasons every quarter. Approaching anything fresh, whether you're somewhat familiar with it or not, yields its own joys.

Aren't we all thrilled to start a new school year? Think about the rush of energy you have…not doing the boring stuff like attending meetings and lesson plans, but meeting new students, setting up the classroom, and welcoming the possibilities of new successes. Being able to mold impressionable minds while helping them to see the world beyond

Cadence of Life 75

the scope of their experiences is an undertaking for you as well. Even if your excitement is based on the notion that you are one school year closer to retirement, you've found that something to motivate you. For some teachers, it means using all of the tools that worked best for you in the last stretch to end your career with a bag.

What's even more meaningful is when students and co-workers can see your enthusiasm, that infectious rhythm pumping through your veins. Seeing you teach with passion and fervor makes your students want to learn and be a part of what you're doing. Likewise, it gives you a sense of pride in positively affecting the lives of your pupils. Enthusiasm makes each project, yes even the daunting projects, more fun.

An example of how my enthusiasm as a band instructor rubbed off on my students happened very early in my teaching career. Two years in, a young Fedrick Ingram was the proud band director at Booker T. Washington High School in Overtown, a historic heart of Miami assigned to blacks. When it opened, it was the first high school educating black students south of Palm Beach. While the area thrived with commerce in the early 1900s and is credited as being home to one the first black millionaire of the American South, D. A. Dorsey, as time progressed, the neighborhood went downhill. The nighttime entertainment scene was comparable to the world renowned Miami Beach at its height during the 1940s and 1950s. Wildly popular entertainers including Billie Holiday, Ella Fitzgerald, Count Basie, and Nat King Cole called Overtown a vacation refuge. Similarly, progressive thought leaders such as Zora Neale Hurston and W. E. B. Du Bois spent significant amounts of time in the neighborhood. Even during its heyday, the neighborhood, which was home to the Lyric Theatre, was brimming with black American railroad construction workers who needed 'passes' to cross the bridge to enter middle and upper income white neighborhoods like Coral Gables and Miami Beach.

Serious economic decline spurred from urban renewal and constructing interstate highways including I-95 and the Dolphin Expressway. The neighborhood became fragmented, population dwindled, and as businesses closed and money left the community, the word 'ghetto' became associated with Overtown. The same mentality that prompted blacks to need passes to get into upper income white neighborhoods is what kept many of my Caucasian counterparts from crossing the bridge and encouraging me to do the same. So at this juncture in the story, Overtown has not seen anywhere near the level of prosperity that it had decades prior; quite the opposite. In fact a vast majority of its residents are on some form of government assistance and do not have college educations. Being a Miami native, I used to go over the bridge all of the time. I was familiar with the area and it didn't bother me. So I laughed when my co-workers would tell me to stay away. Until one particular day.

I crossed over the 14th Street Bridge and was stopped by the light. You've seen enough movies and TV shows to predict what I'm going to say next. Out of nowhere, a gun appeared next to my temple and this young man said to me, "If you don't get out of the car, I'm gonna blow your head off."

My first response was to try to talk my way out of this, realizing that I had taken part in this thievery process putting myself out there. There I was, two years into my career, finally making some decent money and was able to buy myself a new vehicle. I chose a black Ford Explorer. I couldn't wait to lace my new baby with 20" rims and TVs in the head rests. I customized it to my liking, down to the license plates. The front plate said 'Maestro,' and my tag holder said 'Bethune-Cookman College' which was the name prior to the school being accredited as a university.

We are all, to an extent, products of our environment. Whether we choose to emulate what we see or rise above that and do the opposite. But if you know anything about Miami culture, we are flashy. So yeah, I had my rims and TVs in my truck. It was all legal, Miami-Dade County School District money. I was on the straight and narrow, so what could it hurt, right?

I knew he could see I was well-dressed in slacks, a button down, and tie. "Hey man, I teach right over there at the high school." He did not want to hear that, "Man get yo' ass out the car!" I hopped out, he hopped in. In the blazing Miami sun, I ran back to the school to report what had happened. Running back across the 14th Street Bridge, I knew I was never going to see my truck again. I kicked myself in the butt with every stride, blaming myself for being so flashy knowing what area of town I was going to every day.

The seriousness of the situation really hit me as I arrived back to the school. I'd literally just had a gun put to my head. At any point, during the brief altercation, if I'd said the wrong thing or moved too swiftly, my mom would have had to bury me. By the time the police arrived, I was really shaken up. I just couldn't believe I had been carjacked! I didn't bother anyone, that's not something that should have happened to me.

The next day, I was summoned to the front office where I saw the police who'd taken my statement the day before. Walking up to him, I couldn't figure out why he seemed to be so giddy. As he saw me approaching, he boomed, "You're not going to believe this! We found your car this morning!" I'm sure my mouth flew open. I'd lived in Miami long enough to know what happened to cars once they were forcibly separated from their owners. Finding it was not enough for me if it was going to be sitting on bricks and stripped, meaning they'd taken the tires and rims off along with everything of value from its interior. A shell of a vehicle was not going to do this Florida boy from the hood any good.

His next words caught me by surprise. "There's not a scratch on it. Everything is intact, the exact way you left it. We even recovered your wallet and it still has money in it!" I was completely dumbfounded. How was I plucked from my truck at gun point and there was not a scratch on it or anything missing from it?

Come to find out, a band student intervened. He was a young man who, like me, grew up in the hood. He was one of the kids everybody knew not to mess with because he was gang affiliated. His older brother had a car ring that stole, stripped, and sold cars. When he saw the truck with my custom plates, he went off. Over the next few days, I heard this story from multiple sources. From all accounts, the gist of it is, when my student saw my truck in the shop at 2 o'clock in the morning getting ready to be stripped down, he exploded. "Where the hell did y'all get this truck?" From my understanding, my student completely cursed out the guy who carjacked me. My student told the guy to take the car and leave it somewhere it could be found and it better not have a scratch on it.

After hearing this, I approached the student to ask him if what I was hearing was indeed true. He brushed me off saying, "I can't really talk about that. It is what it is, but I want you to know that won't happen again." To this day, we have never talked about it, he was adamant about that. He went on to graduate and gave all the credit to the band program. He said he could care less about a high school diploma, he just wanted to be in the band. He was involved in all kinds of illegal and morally corrupt activities…except for the three hours he was with me in band practice. To this day, we remain really good friends.

My love and enthusiasm for band generated a love and enthusiasm for band in him. He truly felt that. If I approached my job with meek, half-hearted efforts, that is exactly what I would have gotten back. If my band class was boring and left my students feeling like they didn't accomplish anything, they wouldn't want to be a part of my program. Enthusiasm is like flipping a switch; the end result is reached more easily than if approached with a lackluster attitude.

A teacher's approach can make a huge difference in the way your class receives information. You being enthusiastic about standing in front of them will help them to be motivated and engaged as they learn. The importance of enthusiasm can't be stressed enough. Now, all teachers don't necessarily have overly bubbly dispositions, but that doesn't mean you can't approach instruction with zest and charisma.

Know that your energy as a teacher is contagious. If you look at students sitting around your classroom like 'another day, another paycheck,' their response will be in kind. However, if you welcome them in wanting to teach, nurturing relationships, and being genuinely invested in their achievement, they will match your strong desire with a desire to learn.

Wouldn't you want to be the reason their grades improve? Wouldn't you feel good if you helped motivate their eagerness to be more studious? Declining academic performance is directly related to student engagement. Whether the student is extrinsically motivated, where learning is a means to an end as in grades, performances, and projects, or intrinsically motivated, learning to satisfy curiosity, mastery, and enjoyment, the goal is to positively influence your students to learn – and do so successfully.

Looking for ways to add enthusiasm into your day is not a difficult task. When others see how enthusiastic you are about a subject, it is likely their responses will be positive.

Do what you love. Of course every task will have parts of it that you prefer not to have to deal with. Don't focus on those. Instead, focus on the more positive aspects of the job. A sense of enthusiasm will come naturally because you will be doing something you really want to do.

Keep learning. Remember I spoke about excitement surrounding the 'new'? When you dig a little deeper into your craft, you are learning more techniques and strategies to help you be more efficient at teaching. In doing so, the newness will spawn more enthusiasm.

Find other enthusiasts. Moods are contagious. Nobody wants to be around Debbie Downer because, well, she's always down and constantly points out the negative of each situation. Finding a few kindred souls who also project enthusiasm about what they do will rub off on you.

Like any other skill in your educational toolkit, enthusiasm must be exercised. Think about the difference you could make as an enthusiastic teacher. Look back at the story you just read. If I had not made a genuine impression on that band student, the story would have had a different, less favorable ending. If he had not connected with me in the band room, not only would he not have cared enough to even notice that my truck was on the chopping block, but he may not have graduated high school. As you cultivate your enthusiasm for teaching, think about the difference you are making in young lives.

Name three people who show enthusiasm in what they do.

_____

_____

_____

How do they each show their enthusiasm?

_____

_____

_____

What are ways you can also show enthusiasm for your craft?

_____

_____

_____

_____

_____

CHAPTER 6

dedication

NOUN

ded·i·ca·tion

\ˌde-di-ˈkā-shən\

: self-sacrificing devotion and loyalty

"Dedicate some of your life to others. Your dedication will not be a sacrifice. It will be an exhilarating experience because it is an intense effort applied toward a meaningful end."

- DR. THOMAS DOOLEY

Dedication seems to be one of those words that has been used, overused, and abused so much its meaning has been watered down. By definition, dedication means to be wholly committed to something, as to an ideal, political cause, or personal goal. If there is something you want to do, you must be dedicated to seeing it through. Sounds easy enough, right? But what about when you come against difficulties? When mountains, physical or emotional complications, arise and you just can't seem to see your way beyond them…what then? You picture the end goal in mind and keep striving, letting dedication lead the way.

Some wins come quick and easy, while others take grit and lots of time. Dedication is not something that will be exercised on the quick easy wins, oh no. This personal development tool gets its workout on the long roads. You see, dedication is a form of commitment. There is no commitment in something that is easily accomplished. How could there be? If it didn't take much time or effort, then there was nothing to commit to. Practicing dedication comes from feeling losses, yet insisting on a win; receiving setbacks, still pushing toward goals; and going up against opposition, however, driving forward.

Before I dive into my story of how dedication led to success, perhaps a couple stories of familiar names will help to illustrate the practice. Tyler Perry, actor, writer, producer, and director, easily recognizable in his Madea get-up put on his first play for seven years with nobody showing up. The loss to his pockets and his ego did not deter him, he continued to dedicate the resources needed to bring audiences to him. Thomas Edison, discovered the lightbulb after an exhausting 10,000 plus attempts coining the popular quote, "I have not failed. I've just found 10,000 ways that won't work." Walt Disney was fired from a job for not being creative enough, then one of his first business ventures, Laugh-o-Gram Studios went bankrupt. The creator of The Happiest Place on Earth did not let those bumps in the road stop him; he was determined to put smiles on the faces of millions, which he ultimately has done through animations, movies, and wildly-successful theme parks.

When I think of my own personal journey, one story of dedication exceeds the others, my first year as a band director at Miami Carol City High School, home to the Marching Chiefs. It was the most tumultuous year I've ever had teaching. This school had never had a band director who wasn't from Florida A&M University (FAMU) and the Marching Chiefs date back to 1963. The Carol City Chiefs are arguably the best band in the city, even to this day.

When I got the job, there was a complete uproar, "What the what? From where?" The not-so-quiet murmurings of the students and parents were totally against me from day one. Being from the rival HBCU, Bethune-Cookman, I had the hardest time ever trying to implement anything. You see, in Florida there are four HBCUs, but two of these schools have one of the biggest rivalries in the country. The two main institutions of higher education the black community attends, are BCU and FAMU. And it's been like that for generations.

If you don't live in the south, it may be difficult for you to understand the importance of a school's band, especially the marching band. Football and halftime are king in Florida, particularly in black communities. The source of pride and inspiration of our community could be seen on full display every Friday and Saturday at what we in Miami call 'the mecca' Traz Powell Stadium.

The thought that I, a BCU Wildcat, had taken their FAMU Rattler band director's job was unthinkable. So word on the street was that I'd gotten the job because I knew somebody; I also heard that I was a relative of the principle, LOL. Another rumor was that my previous school wanted to get rid of me. None of these claims were true. I interviewed and landed the job at age 28 with my director's baton in hand. As you can see I didn't have a fair shake from minute one.

About a month after I'd been working there, I was at band practice on the field. From where the field was located, you could not see the parking lot. So here I am directing this awesome, sizable group of 250 band students at Miami Carol City High. When the auxiliary team came in from rehearsing on the other side of the school, my dance team sponsor came over to me and said, "Ingram we need to talk." I was in the middle of band practice, which I did not like being disturbed for a number of reasons. It threw me off my game and broke the concentration of the students. You have to get into a flow to practice band. That flow is made of cadences, melodies, and scales that seem to transcend you to a whole different stratosphere. You see, when you are in that flow, you don't want it to be interrupted. Especially if you're working on a problem area that you are just…about…to…fix. Falling back to earth from the musical oasis can be difficult to recover from.

She said, "Something's wrong with your car."

I suspiciously asked, "How do you know that something is wrong with my car? What are you talking about?"

"They have vandalized your car and you need to get over there right now!" I told the kids to march in, ran over to see my car and lost it. They spray painted my car orange and green, FAMU's colors. It happened during band practice because that's the only time they could guarantee I wouldn't see them do it. I nearly lost my mind and the kids nearly lost their lives that day. The security officer had to hold me back, but I went off like nobody's business. I turned from Bruce Banner into The Incredible Hulk.

I knew it was the band students because I was trying to implement a few things into the program that I thought would be of a great benefit. No matter what I brought, they thought it was from BCU so they acted as though it came from a different country, like I was speaking a foreign language to them. Any change I brought about, they would fight me tooth and nail.

My first year as their band director, from my perspective, was walking into a dynamic band program to make it phenomenal! You know the adage, 'good, better, best'? Well, I was walking in beyond that. So, I found new adjectives for it like impressive, dynamic, phenomenal.

It was so tough that year. The very next year, my colleagues saw the hell that I had been going through to ramp up the program; they appreciated my attitude of sticking with it and not giving up or looking down at my students. They made me the school's teacher of the year. From there, my career really took off. I became the Miami-Dade County Teacher of the Year. To put this in perspective, this skinny, stutterer raised in a poor household in the hood was being recognized as the best teacher in the county! The feeling of nostalgia reminded me of when I became a drum major at BCU! Rising through the ranks of the band to essentially lead the band on and off the field was a tremendous feeling.

Hopefully, now you see why this story comes to mind when discussing dedication. Overcoming the adversity of leaving my parents to attend BCU, being hungry, or wearing beat-up, holey shoes were things I anticipated and had a plan of recourse to help me succeed. Going into a large, well-developed band program whose students and parents wanted anybody other than a BCU graduate was not anything I could have been prepared for.

My driving force for wanting to stick with it instead of transfer out was because I was dedicated. I was not going to let anybody run me away. I never went into anything with the thought process that I would quit; I was determined not to be defeated. I'd seen and learned a lot from my days walking through the halls at BCU. Similarly, I learned a lot from people I respected and admired. Throughout my life, there were echoes of 'keep doing it until you get it right' that reverberated through my mind. Quitting was not an option I ever considered.

Instead, I focused on when it was going to get better. I prayed a lot and did my thing; it all worked out in the end. Nobody goes into anything expecting to fail. If you expect to fail, you might as well not even try, right? This is what happens when people have dreams or goals that ultimately die because they anticipate the failure and thus don't put forth the effort. These students at Carol City wanted to win! I had gone into an established band program. The band not being successful was a reflection on them, as well as me because we all took such pride in it. They didn't want to look bad to their friends and neighbors. I didn't want to look like I came into the band program and failed. The pride of the Carol City Chiefs Marching Band was at stake for us all.

I was determined to win and more determined to make an impact. I became invested in them personally. How can you make more of an impact while being dedicated to your students? Here are the steps I took.

I devoted time in their personal lives. I began taking an interest in who they were. If a kid had other interests, such as basketball, then I'd go to basketball games. If they volunteered at the local park, then I'd volunteer at the local park. I bailed kids out of jail and went to bat for them. Every other Saturday, we'd have basketball games with each other. I made the kids fall in-love, not only with me, but with the program itself. They saw that

I was not just interested in my program, but in them as people.

I proved to be resourceful toward future ambitions. On another level, they started getting scholarships to college. Yes, I sent kids away on scholarships to FAMU and BCU, but I sent more students away on scholarships than the program had ever seen before. The second year I was there, 35 students earned scholarships to a myriad of colleges, but mostly FAMU and BCU. These students were amazing musicians, what they lacked was understanding that higher education was serious academic business. In order to get to college, they had to take care of business academically at the high school level first. Once I realized where the disconnect was, I implemented study halls and Saturday sessions to help them. They saw that I wanted them to win, just as much if not more than they did.

I created a family. I took them to church. At the beginning of marching season, I'd ask a pastor to accept our band family and offer up a prayer for us before school started. Over the eight years I was there, we went to five different churches. It wasn't mandatory for the students; but they welcomed the opportunity. Close to 250 of them would get dressed up in their Sunday's best to go to church with me.

Those are the types of things that helped them understand who I was, as well as who they were. So the internal feud they had within themselves stemming from my alma mater fell to the wayside as they saw that I was only there to do my job…turn dynamic into phenomenal.

What are two things that others who know you would say you are dedicated to?

_____
_____

How do you display your dedication?

_____
_____
_____
_____
_____

Name two ways you think you have positively influenced others based on answers from the first question.

_____
_____
_____
_____
_____
_____
_____

CHAPTER 7

initiative

ADJECTIVE

ini·tia·tive

\ i-'ni-shə-tiv \

: energy or aptitude displayed in initiation of action

"Success depends in a very large measure upon individual initiative and exertion and cannot be achieved except by a dint of hard work."

- ANNA PAVLOVA

Initiative is an art form. It's all about taking charge, showing a willingness to take ownership or responsibility. If you want to get something done, you must take initiative. As with any goal you hope to achieve, or milestone you aim to reach, initiative is paramount in your personal growth. Where professional development is concerned, this principle separates the talkers from the doers. You know who talkers are, the ones who make plans, talk about what grandiose projects they want to undertake without showing a shred of action or devising a plan for follow-through.

Initiative is a core character builder, one that shows who knows how to grind it out or isn't afraid to do the work. Through the process of getting your hands dirty, you grow as an individual, as well as in what you are able to offer.

Employers love to see employees who show initiative. When you are able to take ownership to get things done, that attitude strongly correlates to you being a leader. Leaders see what needs to be done and make sure that it gets done. Think about some of the influential people you have met in your life. These people may be teachers, church members, community leaders, or positively memorable management from your job. What made their impact more substantial than others? Were they being selfless by dedicating their energies to a cause or a team of people? Were they instrumental in finding new solutions to problems that seemed not to go away? Did they speak out about injustices or double standards? Were they able to rightfully acknowledge people on their team?

My road to initiative came on behalf of my students. The hardest professional decision I've had to make was whether or not to leave the classroom. Going into teaching that was my plan, to teach. The thought of not teaching band full-time had not crossed my mind. Music is my passion; it's my love. I was blessed to recognize the beauty of working in a field that I am passionate about. After seeing how the system treated kids, I felt motivated to do more.

The pivotal moment for me came learning, yet not understanding how the State of Florida detained students because they couldn't pass tests. Not because they weren't passing classes, but because they couldn't pass the state exam. I watched kids drop out of school with this being the only block to their high school diploma. That lit a fire under me.

I, too, came from a less than privileged background and knew that for some of these kids, this would be one of their lives' greatest accomplishments.

I took the initiative to get real answers and seek change by asking my union representatives and administrators, "Why is the state allowed to get away with this? This is a good kid, they've done all of the work, passed all of their classes, and because they can't pass the state test, we aren't going to give them a diploma?" It didn't make sense to me. Questions turned into attending school board meetings, committee meetings, asking questions to administrators higher up on the food chain. Because of the activism and people who were also interested in the knowledge that I had as a practitioner and a classroom teacher, I was able to get deeper and deeper.

Soon I was asked to go to workshops and put on presentations. Before you know it, I was head over heels into it being asked to run for union leader. At that point, I had to make a decision if I was going to remain in the classroom or travel down a road that would remove me from the classroom, but that would allow me to help students in much more of a profound way. While it was difficult not to see students every day, knowing the types of changes I would have a voice to see implemented meant more to me and ultimately to them. I've seen kids stuck in classes they shouldn't have been in, not enough or incorrect textbooks; even in my department the band equipment was broken. I took the initiative to stand up and say something about the neglect and unfairness that I was seeing.

I don't regret my decision to become an advocate at all. I still have a heart for music, I have a passion for band, and I help out in different classrooms and with programs every chance I get. I think leaving the classroom was the right decision because you need people who are willing to speak up on behalf of the students. That's what it takes to get anything done on the county and state levels. You have to be willing to speak truth, use your voice in confidence; you have to know the arguments and know public policy. I've learned so much about laws, lawmaking, and public policy throughout this journey. That knowledge has not only empowered me to make changes, but it has also permitted me to empower others.

I absolutely love what I do. I never would have thought that I'd have this level of influence in the state or the country. I'm passionate about striving every day to make a difference as it relates to kids and schools.

When I was elected as the President of the United Teachers of Dade (County) teachers' union, I was the first African-American to hold that position. That was a huge milestone for me. It's always remarkable to be celebrated in the community, being the first black anything, even into the 2000s in a tremendous feat. Subsequently, I was elected Vice President then President of the Florida Education Association (FEA).

Throughout these amazing opportunities to learn and grow, I've come to be known for organizing people and unifying communities on pressing issues. Similar to the way I was able to become one with the band at Miami Carol City coming from a rival college to that of where the former band director came from, as a social advocate I have a knack for bringing together groups of people who have comparable interests. My mission for even leaving the classroom was to help create equity in schools, primarily those serving black and brown students. I lobby to have the same types of programs, same quality teachers, equal funding, and resources in schools regardless of the zip code. Children should not be victims of circumstance. It is their right in the public education system to have the same opportunities available to them without their impoverished way of life being restrictive.

I've done significant work traveling the country helping parents organize themselves to go to school board meetings to start intelligible conversations about not having the proper programs or not having the proper funding. I've worked with social organizations from the NAACP to the National Action Network, as well as environmental groups. My activism is to help people of color articulate their issues as they relate to demanding fairness everywhere from local politicians to school boards.

If you want to see change, you must take initiative. By reading *Cadence of Life*, you have already proven that you are ready to take initiative on some level. Now, pair that initiative with creativity and you are ready to change your world.

Change is good. If you continue to do things the way they have always been done, the results will also continue to be the same. Search for effective solutions and new approaches to pulling responsiveness out of your students.

Share your ideas. Have you ever been in a faculty meeting and someone speaks up to share their idea, which is similar to yours, that winds up being a success? Were you upset that they got to bask in the glory of the outcome and you couldn't? Well, if you had spoken up, you would have too. Your brilliant ideas aren't worth anything if you don't share them, so open up!

Consider every opportunity. Opportunities for growth lie within just about every situation, so ask yourself, 'What can I learn from this?' Asking yourself this question is taking the initiative to challenge yourself and your own status quo. If at first you don't find the answer, ask yourself repeatedly until you are able to carve out a benefit to show your professional abilities. Discover the possibilities for new career moves to open up.

Ask questions…like I did. When something doesn't make sense to you or you want to gain a deeper understanding, ask questions. Observe your surroundings as much as possible, then be openly curious about the processes taking place and new standards that are in existence. As you analyze the new information coming to you, it will give rise to fresh ideas of ways you can contribute to your organization.

Taking initiative opens doors. It helps you see more opportunities to grow as a person and as a professional. More importantly, showing initiative lets others see what an asset you can be to their organization. Think about ways you can initiate change where you are. Don't be afraid; jump out there to make a change!

What initiatives have you pioneered?

_____

_____

What did you do to get them into motion?

_____

_____

_____

What were the results?

_____

_____

_____

_____

How could the results have been more impactful?

_____

_____

CHAPTER 8

disruption

NOUN

dis·rup·tive

/dɪsˈrʌpʃn/

: to break apart

: to interrupt the normal course or unity of

"We shouldn't be afraid to be disruptive – we should be in charge of our own disruption."

- ALBERTO AGUAYO

The word disruption is frequently used in reference to both the classroom and business. In the classroom, students disrupt instruction by tapping pencils, talking amongst themselves, note passing, or chair rocking. Students engage in low-level disruption that interferes with instruction in such a way where the teacher has the responsibility of addressing the problematic behavior to maintain a civil, orderly environment. Thankfully, the disruption is usually not dramatic enough to bring instruction to a complete halt. Looking at the term in this way, it is seen as a negative, something that causes disorder.

Now on the business side, disruption is a happening, a grand occurrence within a standing business model or industry. Clayton M. Christensen, an American scholar, defined and analyzed the term 'disruptive innovation' in 1995 and it was deemed the most influential business idea of the 21st century. Not all innovations are disruptive, even if the contribution seems to be revolutionary.

For example, in the late 19th century the first automobiles hit the scene. However, this was not disruptive because they were so expensive that many Americans couldn't afford them. Some 30 years later when Ford's Model Ts began mass production trying to keep up with consumer demand, this caused a disruption being that the price was so affordable automobiles were commonly replacing the horse-and-buggy. Disruptions are ripples that innovators have found a way to turn into tides of positive change.

Looking at it from a constructive aspect, disruption is all about growth. Everyone tries to be different and works hard to distinguish themselves from others; but that presents a challenge when you use comparison as a motivational tool.

A part of my role as a union advocate is not accepting the status quo; not accepting things as they are. We have to move the needle for anything, not only in schools and with our children, but in life. Sometimes that requires disrupting the status quo of your life. Congressman John Lewis talks about getting in good trouble, making moves towards what is right. So, back to the automobile example, disruption can certainly be a good thing!

When I became union president, we hadn't gotten significant raises in a number of years in Miami-Dade County Schools. I felt I needed to do something to disrupt what I thought was a bad avenue for us to go down. As soon as I became union president, I began putting out flyers and making personal contact with people in an effort to drum up support from thousands of teachers, administrators, and staff to shut down a major thoroughfare of Miami known as Biscayne Boulevard. The reason I did this was to bring awareness to the way we were handling things as an organization. We needed to do things differently. We needed to let people know we were there, on the scene, and not going to 'take no wooden nickels' as my grandmother used to say. Basically, that meant we were not going to just allow ourselves to be treated any ol' kind of way. As a young leader stepping into the role of union president directing over 30,000 educators in Miami-Dade County, I knew I would be disrupting the way the school system handled business.

The disruption I initiated was a bold step that had not been done since 1968. The Florida statewide teachers' strike of 1968 encompassed the months of February and March. It was a strike action by teachers and other education workers belonging to the Florida Education Association (FEA). At a time when low wages and decreasing benefits met a sharp rise in attendance, the strike was meant to bring attention to underfunding of the state-wide school system. The strike ranged from days in some counties to three months in others. A special Florida legislature was held to vote on higher taxes to ramp up more funding. While the elevated tax proposal was approved, FEA members voted to keep striking as they felt the funding hikes were not substantial enough. No additional funding was forthcoming however, so ultimately, the FEA settled their contracts and went back to work by March.

During the strike, two-thirds of the county's educators walked out gathering at Miami Marine Stadium overlooking Biscayne Bay. It was in the same spirit over 40 years later that we stood on Biscayne Boulevard, in almost the exact location, fighting for the same thing, more respectable pay.

There was a great amount of effort in organizing and building relationships in the community. The process was very, very tense, but also very rewarding. It gave me the satisfaction of wanting to advance an issue and recognize the importance of how improving it could affect myself and others. To see the results we needed, I knew we had to go a different path from what had been done before. That was a pivotal moment for me, understanding the power of blazing a trail to incite change rather than follow behind the footsteps of others who wanted higher pay, but did not want to disrupt the standard to get what they wanted.

Our personal lives are very much the same in that way. It takes courage, integrity, and getting things done through the proper channels to see change. Along the way you will run into obstacles, but that will happen whether you are causing the disruption, or just lying back riding the tides.

If you wait on the person next to you to cause a disruption in their own life or job circumstances, you are going about this all wrong. You have to recognize that there are changes to be made in your life, then be intentional about the work you do and the energy you put out to address and improve your situation.

It all begins with your mindset. I had the mindset that educators needed, and deserved, better pay. I'd seen calendar years be torn off with little to no change. Rather than give in to the fear the same situation would continue to happen, I decided to put a plan into action. Could I have done what others ahead of me had done to rectify the problem? Sure! Would it have reaped the results I wanted? Probably not. At least not for a while. If writing letters and making motions had not worked for others, why would I think it would work in my favor? I knew it wouldn't.

A move of this magnitude required a big shake, something huge that would really get the attention of the decision makers. Guess what? The strike shutting down Biscayne Boulevard worked!

While your problem may not require thousands of people to partner with to find a solution, you could probably still use a disruption in your own career. The tools that I've given you in this book will help you align your passion with purpose, enthusiasm, and dedication. As long as you keep striving forward, there is no way you can't win.

The word 'disruption' is a transitive verb. Now, let's break this down. Transitive means relating to or characterized by transition. We know transition means change. A verb is a word that expresses an act or mode of being. So a transitive verb means the word describes an 'act of change.'

The question is…what *act* will you commit to *change* your current state of being? Ask yourself the following questions to incite a positive change in your life.

- What situation bothers me most about my life?
- How long have I been dealing with this situation?
- If given the power to change it, would I?
- Do I have the power to change it?
- Why or why not?
- What are three things I could do to alter the situation to be more agreeable to my life?
- What are the steps for each?
- Which avenue would yield the greatest, most desirable results?

Now…put your plan into action!

What area of your life can use a bold change?

_____

_____

_____

What would you like to see different?

_____

_____

_____

How do you plan to make an adjustment?

_____

_____

_____

_____

How can you refresh your mindset when things seem not to be going the way you anticipate?

_____

_____

_____

CHAPTER 9

finale

NOUN

fi·na·le

\ fə-'na-lē

the close or termination of something: such as

a : the last section of an instrumental musical composition

b : the closing part, scene, or number in a public performance

c : the last and often climactic event or item in a sequence

"It takes a village to raise a child."

- AFRICAN PROVERB

There is an African proverb, 'It takes a village to raise a child.' Each and every one of us has to find our place in that village. We all have a role to play and it is our duty to ensure our futures collectively as Americans, as well as humans to find how we are able to push our children forward. Educators can't do it without paraprofessionals, paraprofessionals can't do it without bus drivers, bus drivers can't do it without the cafeteria workers, and the cafeteria workers can't do it without the custodial engineers. In fact, when a school gets money for an 'A' grade, everyone should get paid. Each person in our educational society plays an important role. We must feel good ourselves about the role we play while motivating others to do the same.

Public education, particularly in Florida, needs to move in a different direction. We have seen the adverse impacts of education reform as put forth originally by Jeb Bush, then followed up by Charlie Crist. It is my belief that we need to fundamentally move in a different direction where teachers have more autonomy. Teachers want to teach children, not test them. Every time they teach to the test and the test deviates because of new concepts developed just a few months before the test, the students are thrown off course. Students are growing up not knowing the 3R's, not writing in cursive, not having the intrinsic motivation to analyze and correct situations independently, and have a cadre of things they can't relate to because they are not on the test. God forbid they relocate to another city or state and have to deal with earlier test dates and unfamiliar materials. Bench marks and accountability systems have been punitive for students where they have gotten caught in damaging testing cycles.

As schools are labeled A through F, not only are the schools bearing that grade, but so is the community – families and businesses – teachers, and education professionals in that school. The agenda in education has to be cultivated with the best outcome for the children, as well as those who educate and take care of our children. Public education is comprehensive and must be pushed on those in positions of power to be great.

The *8 Tips* mentioned in this book are here to do just that, give you suggestions on how to ignite a charge in teachers, students, and the governing powers that be toward the betterment of our student population. As an educator, I have worked with students, parents, communities, school boards, and now the state of Florida. After performing in a specific arena for so long, it is easy to get caught in a rut. You get used to a certain way of doing things, it becomes routine. The luster and shine from the beginning stages has dulled over the years. Working has become more of a chore. It's time to change that up. The time is going to pass anyway, might as well have some fun!

Refresh your mind and your approach with these tips.

Love…what you do. Remember why you started. Love for your job is infectious to your students and co-workers.

Motivation…makes learning fun. If you are excited, so will your class be. Motivate them extrinsically and they will begin to take on an intrinsic motivation to becoming better versions of themselves.

Vision…helps you move forward. You must to have a vision for where you want to go in order to be intentional with your words and actions to get you there.

Enthusiasm...is necessary. It helps putting your best foot forward while having a positive attitude about each day.

Dedication...will show. Students and parents alike will see how committed you are to making an impact on the school, the community, and last but not least, the students. This will encourage the students to work harder for you.

Initiative...is something you must take to see change. Change will happen around you or you can initiate the change you want to see. Don't just ride the tide, be a game changer.

Disruption...can certainly be positive. Disrupt your teaching style and classroom performance by educating yourself with new, fresh techniques and making students feel more engaged.

You are helping to mold the world! Don't forget it. Together, we can all improve the state of education.

Invite Dr. Fedrick Ingram to speak to your organization!

www.ingramcontent.com/pod-product-compliance
Lightning Source LLC
Chambersburg PA
CBHW071131090426
42736CB00012B/2092